Edward
And
The Ladybird

By

Lucy Nunnery

Dedication

For Edward, who makes me smile every day

Acknowledgments

I have to start by thanking Amazon publishing for agreeing to publish my book and the team that worked on putting it all together; it was a fun, creative process from start to finish.

I would also like to thank my illustrator Sarah Peacock who was a joy to work with. She understood the vision I had for the book and worked hard to make the story come alive through the illustrations.

I would lastly like to thank my family and friends for their support on this project, in particular, my mum, whose input and opinion I valued most, and my Auntie Ann, whose encouragement meant a great deal to me.

About the Author

Lucy Nunnery lives in Surrey. Edward and the Ladybird is her first children's book, she is currently working on a sequel to this story.

Edward was a cat that lived in a flat,

He slept most of the day and liked to sit on his mat.

While his owners were at work he'd play with his toys,

Eat lots of snacks and always wait patiently for them

to come back.

One day just by chance, Edward looked up
and glanced at a ladybird on the windowsill.

He tapped with his paw, then looked up
and saw the ladybird flying in through the door.

"Hello my name is Edward, and I'm a house cat. I saw you outside, do you fancy a chat?"

"Hi, my name is Lily, the ladybird said, how do you do? It would be lovely to chat with you."

"We have something in common,
we both have black spots, but yours are like smudges,
and mine are like dots!"

"Wow, giggled Edward, we could be twins, we're two of
a kind! So tell me your story, and I'll tell you mine."

"I live in a plant just outside of your window,
It's tall and has leaves, but not any people."

"Don't you have owners the same way I do? That
brings you your food and cuddles you too?"

"No," said Lily, "I live on my own,

It sometimes feels scary to feel so alone."

"I understand," said Edward, "I don't leave this

flat, the world can be a scary place,

and my owners just want to keep me safe."

"They must really care for you," said

Lily, "Keeping you safe and feeding you

too!"

Edward showed Lily around,

"This is where my treats are kept,

there's yummy biscuits, fish,

and my own special little dish," said Edward proudly.

"Wow," said Lily, "I love your mat!"

"It's cosy," said Edward, "Just right for a cat."

"The plant I live in is drafty and cold, not like this, I feel so at home."

"Yes," said Edward, "It's homely and bright, the kind of place you feel just right."

"It's clear you're very loved," said Lily.

"I know you know this too,

with lots of treats and toys to play,

to keep you busy too."

"But being loved as much as I am, can still be lonely too."

Said Edward, "My owners go to work all day,

they don't stay home and play, no

matter how much I wish they'd stay."

"I wish I belonged to someone, somewhere," said Lily,

"I get awfully lonely, it's like nobody cares."

Edward could see Lily was sad, so he made a suggestion
that made her so glad.

"I'd love you to be my friend Lily,
and see you every day,
I'd even share my treats with you
no matter what you say."

"Really" said Lily, "we could be friends?
And Lily's lonely heart soon began to
mend."

So Edward showed Lily his toys, he let her sit on his mat, and she became best friends with Edward, the house cat.

THE END

Ingram Content Group UK Ltd.
Milton Keynes UK
UKHW052114290523
422536UK00006B/18

9 781916 540576